I0164132

A Numerology Series

by

Lloyd Leon

SEVEN

Life Path Seven

Contents

Chapter 1

Understanding Life Path 7

The Significance of Life Path Numbers

The significance of life path numbers extends far beyond mere numerological calculations; they serve as profound indicators of our spiritual journey and personal development. For individuals on the Life Path 7, these numbers illuminate the unique qualities and challenges that define their existence. Life Path 7 individuals are often characterized by their introspective nature, analytical minds, and a deep yearning for spiritual understanding. Recognizing the implications of their life path number can lead to a more profound appreciation of their life experiences and the inherent gifts they possess.

Understanding the significance of Life Path 7 is crucial for personal growth and spiritual enlightenment. This number signifies a quest for knowledge and truth, urging individuals to delve into the mysteries of life and the universe. Those on this path may find themselves drawn to philosophical inquiries and spiritual practices that promote self-discovery. By embracing the essence of Life Path 7, individuals can unlock their potential and harness their innate abilities, paving the way for a fulfilling journey towards enlightenment and self-actualization.

In terms of career and calling, Life Path 7 individuals often excel in roles that allow for independence, creativity, and deep thinking. They are naturally inclined towards research, writing, and spiritual guidance, where their analytical skills and intuitive insights can shine. Understanding the significance of their life path number can guide them in aligning their career choices with their true calling, ensuring that their professional endeavors resonate with their inner selves. This alignment not only fosters career satisfaction but also enhances their overall sense of purpose.

Relationships for Life Path 7 individuals can be intricate, as they often require deep emotional connections and intellectual stimulation. The significance of their life path number lies in its ability to reveal compatibility dynamics with others. By recognizing their own needs and the needs of their partners, Life Path 7 individuals can cultivate healthier and more meaningful relationships. Understanding the nuances of their emotional intelligence helps them navigate interpersonal challenges, fostering deeper connections grounded in mutual respect and understanding.

Finally, the significance of Life Path 7 encompasses the importance of health and wellness practices tailored to their unique characteristics. Those on this path benefit from meditation, mindfulness, and other holistic approaches that nurture their introspective nature. By incorporating these practices into their daily routines, Life Path 7 individuals can enhance their emotional well-being, balance their introverted tendencies, and engage more fully with the world around them. Embracing the significance of their life path number ultimately empowers them to transform challenges into opportunities for growth and self-expression.

Characteristics of Life Path 7 Individuals

Life Path 7 individuals are often characterized by their deep introspection and a quest for knowledge that transcends the mundane. They possess a natural inclination toward seeking truth and understanding the mysteries of life, which makes them drawn to philosophical and spiritual pursuits. This innate curiosity not only fuels their personal growth but also positions them as lifelong learners, constantly exploring new ideas and concepts. Their analytical nature allows them to dissect information, leading to profound insights that can benefit themselves and others in their journey toward enlightenment.

Emotional intelligence is another hallmark of Life Path 7 individuals. They tend to be highly sensitive and intuitive, allowing them to connect deeply with their own emotions as well as those of others. This capacity for empathy enables them to navigate relationships with care and understanding, although it can also make them susceptible to emotional overwhelm. Cultivating emotional resilience becomes essential, as it empowers them to harness their sensitivity in constructive ways, fostering healthier interactions and deeper connections in their personal and professional lives.

In terms of creativity and expression, Life Path 7 individuals often exhibit a unique blend of originality and introspection.

Their imaginative minds thrive in environments that encourage creative exploration, whether through art, writing, or other forms of self-expression. This creative outlet serves as a powerful tool for processing their thoughts and feelings, offering a channel for them to communicate their insights and experiences. By embracing their creativity, they can unlock new dimensions of their inner selves while inspiring others around them.

Despite their many strengths, Life Path 7 individuals face challenges that require deliberate effort to overcome. Their tendency toward introversion can lead to feelings of isolation, particularly if they struggle to balance their need for solitude with the demands of social engagement. Recognizing the value of connection while honoring their need for introspection is crucial. Developing strategies to engage in social situations without compromising their inner peace allows them to cultivate a fulfilling social life that supports their overall well-being.

Health and wellness practices play a significant role in the lives of Life Path 7 individuals, who often benefit from routines that promote both physical and mental health. Regular meditation, mindfulness exercises, and nature-based activities can enhance their spiritual and emotional states. Such practices not only help in grounding their often restless minds but also facilitate a deeper connection to their inner selves. By prioritizing their health and wellness, Life Path 7 individuals can navigate their journey with greater clarity, balance, and purpose, ultimately unlocking their full potential in all facets of life.

The Spiritual Journey of Life Path 7

The spiritual journey of individuals on Life Path 7 is characterized by a profound quest for knowledge and deeper understanding. Those on this path often find themselves drawn to the mysteries of life, seeking answers to existential questions that lead them to explore various philosophical, spiritual, and metaphysical realms. This journey is not merely about acquiring knowledge; it is about transforming that knowledge into wisdom. Life Path 7 encourages individuals to develop a strong inner life, fostering a connection with their intuition and inner voice, which serves as a compass guiding them through their spiritual exploration.

As Life Path 7 individuals delve into their spiritual journey, they often encounter moments of introspection that challenge their beliefs and perceptions. These experiences can lead to periods of solitude, where they may feel the need to withdraw from the noise of the external world. This introspective phase is essential, as it allows for self-reflection and a deeper understanding of their purpose. Embracing solitude can lead to significant breakthroughs, as it is often in these quiet moments that the most profound insights emerge. The ability to navigate these periods of introspection is a vital aspect of their spiritual growth.

Meditation and mindfulness practices play a crucial role in the spiritual journey of Life Path 7 individuals. These practices help cultivate a sense of inner peace and clarity, enabling them to connect more deeply with their higher selves. By engaging in regular meditation, Life Path 7 individuals can enhance their emotional intelligence, allowing them to process their feelings and experiences more effectively. This not only aids in personal development but also fosters healthier relationships with others, as they become more attuned to their emotions and the emotions of those around them.

The spiritual journey of Life Path 7 also involves embracing creativity and expression as vital components of their growth. This path encourages individuals to explore artistic outlets that resonate with their inner truth, whether through writing, art, or other forms of creative expression. Engaging in creative pursuits allows Life Path 7 individuals to channel their insights and experiences into something tangible, fostering a deeper connection to their spiritual selves. As they express their creativity, they often find that it serves as a powerful tool for healing and self-discovery.

Finally, the challenges faced by Life Path 7 individuals are often steeped in the tension between their inner world and the expectations of the outer world. Learning to balance their introverted nature with the demands of social engagement is a significant aspect of their journey. By recognizing and addressing these challenges, Life Path 7 individuals can cultivate resilience and adaptability, ultimately leading to a more fulfilling and enriched spiritual life. This journey is not merely about overcoming obstacles; it is about embracing the lessons that these challenges provide, allowing for transformative growth and a deeper connection to the spiritual essence of life.

Chapter 2

Unlocking the Potential of Life Path 7

Recognizing Unique Gifts and Talents

Recognizing the unique gifts and talents of individuals on Life Path 7 is crucial for their spiritual growth and overall fulfillment. Life Path 7 individuals are often characterized by their deep introspection, analytical nature, and quest for knowledge. These traits enable them to connect with their inner selves and explore the mysteries of life. However, the challenge lies in acknowledging and embracing these inherent abilities. By doing so, they can unlock their potential and navigate their spiritual journey with confidence.

One of the primary gifts of Life Path 7 is their exceptional ability to analyze and understand complex concepts. This analytical mindset allows them to see patterns and connections that others might overlook. To harness this talent, they should engage in activities that stimulate their intellect, such as studying philosophy, science, or spirituality. By dedicating time to explore these fields, Life Path 7 individuals can deepen their understanding of themselves and the universe, ultimately enhancing their spiritual enlightenment.

Creativity is another significant aspect of Life Path 7. While they may often lean towards introversion, their imagination is rich and vibrant. This creative energy can manifest in various forms, such as writing, art, or music. Encouraging themselves to express these creative impulses not only provides an emotional outlet but also serves as a means to connect with their higher selves. Engaging in creative activities can also help Life Path 7 individuals find their unique voice and contribute meaningfully to the world around them.

Emotional intelligence is a vital component of Life Path 7's journey. Their sensitivity and introspective nature allow them to empathize deeply with others, yet they may struggle with expressing their feelings. Recognizing this gift and actively working on emotional expression can lead to more fulfilling relationships and a better understanding of themselves. Practicing mindfulness and meditation can enhance their emotional awareness and help them navigate interpersonal dynamics with greater ease and compassion.

To truly recognize and embrace their unique gifts, Life Path 7 individuals must also confront their challenges. Often, they may feel misunderstood or isolated due to their introspective tendencies. Acknowledging these feelings and seeking support from like-minded individuals can foster a sense of community and belonging. By sharing their experiences and insights, they can uplift one another and create an environment conducive to personal growth.

Ultimately, recognizing their unique gifts and talents is a vital step toward achieving balance and harmony in all aspects of life.

Embracing Intuition and Inner Wisdom

Embracing intuition and inner wisdom is essential for individuals on the Life Path 7 journey, as it aligns with their natural inclinations toward introspection and spiritual exploration. Life Path 7 individuals often possess a profound inner voice that guides them through life's complexities. Tuning into this intuitive faculty can lead to greater self-awareness and clarity in decision-making. By cultivating a practice that allows for quiet reflection, such as meditation or journaling, Life Path 7s can enhance their ability to listen to their inner guidance, which often provides insights that logical reasoning may overlook.

Developing intuition is not merely about passive listening; it involves actively engaging with one's feelings and thoughts. Life Path 7 individuals can benefit from exploring various techniques that foster this connection, such as mindfulness practices, dream analysis, and visualization exercises. These methods encourage a deeper understanding of emotional responses and the messages they convey. As they learn to trust their instincts, Life Path 7s can navigate personal and professional challenges with a sense of confidence that arises from within, transforming uncertainty into opportunities for growth.

In the context of relationships, embracing intuition is particularly valuable for Life Path 7 individuals, who may sometimes struggle with emotional expression. By connecting with their inner wisdom, they can cultivate stronger and more authentic connections with others. Intuitive insights can guide them in identifying compatible partners and nurturing relationships that resonate with their spiritual values. Furthermore, this heightened awareness can assist in recognizing when relationships no longer serve their highest good, enabling them to make choices that align with their true selves.

Career choices for Life Path 7 individuals often benefit from a strong reliance on intuition. Many find fulfillment in roles that allow for creativity, analysis, and independent thought. By embracing their inner wisdom, they can identify opportunities that align with their passions and skills, leading to a career path that feels authentic and rewarding. Whether it's through consulting, research, or creative endeavors, Life Path 7s can harness their intuitive insights to carve out a profession that not only satisfies their intellectual curiosity but also resonates with their spiritual journey.

Ultimately, the journey of embracing intuition and inner wisdom is a transformative one for Life Path 7 individuals. It empowers them to navigate life with a deeper understanding of themselves and their place in the world. By cultivating a relationship with their inner voice, they can unlock their full potential, leading to a life rich in spiritual growth, fulfilling relationships, and meaningful careers. This alignment with their intuitive self fosters resilience, enabling them to overcome obstacles and embrace the challenges that come their way, ultimately guiding them toward a path of enlightenment and self-discovery.

The Role of Solitude in Personal Growth

The role of solitude in personal growth is particularly significant for individuals on Life Path 7, as it aligns closely with their innate tendencies toward introspection and self-discovery. Solitude provides an essential space for reflection, allowing Life Path 7 individuals to delve deep into their thoughts and feelings. This introspective journey can lead to greater self-awareness, enabling them to understand their motivations, fears, and desires. In a world that often prioritizes external connections and social engagement, carving out time for solitude becomes not just a luxury but a necessity for meaningful growth.

In moments of solitude, Life Path 7 individuals can explore their spiritual beliefs and practices more profoundly. Such exploration often leads to a clearer understanding of their life's purpose and the unique gifts they possess. Meditation, a practice particularly relevant for this life path, serves as a powerful tool during these solitary times. Through meditation, individuals can access deeper states of consciousness, fostering spiritual insights that are pivotal for their journey. This process not only enhances their spiritual growth but also nurtures emotional intelligence, as they learn to navigate their inner landscapes with compassion and clarity.

Solitude also plays a crucial role in enhancing creativity and expression, traits that are often pronounced in Life Path 7 individuals. When alone, they can engage in creative pursuits without the distractions of social obligations or external expectations. This freedom allows for the emergence of authentic ideas and artistic expressions, which can be incredibly fulfilling. The creative process often requires a quiet space where the mind can wander and explore. By embracing solitude, Life Path 7 individuals can unlock their creative potential, leading to new avenues in their personal and professional lives.

The challenges that Life Path 7 individuals may face, such as balancing their introverted nature with social engagements, can be navigated more effectively through periods of solitude. These moments provide the necessary time to recharge and reflect, enabling them to return to social situations with renewed energy and perspective. Additionally, solitude allows for the processing of interpersonal dynamics and relationships, leading to healthier interactions when they do engage with others. Understanding the importance of this balance can significantly enhance both their emotional well-being and their relationships.

Ultimately, solitude serves as a transformative catalyst for personal growth among Life Path 7 individuals. It offers a sanctuary for introspection, creativity, and spiritual development. By consciously integrating solitude into their lives, they can cultivate a deeper understanding of themselves and their place in the world. This journey not only enriches their personal experiences but also empowers them to share their unique gifts more authentically with others, fulfilling their potential as intuitive seekers and spiritual guides.

Chapter 3

Spiritual Growth and Life Path 7

The Search for Deeper Meaning

The quest for deeper meaning is a defining characteristic of those on Life Path 7. This journey often leads to introspection and a profound search for understanding life's mysteries. Life Path 7 individuals possess an innate curiosity that drives them to explore philosophical questions and spiritual truths. As they navigate through life, they seek to uncover the layers of existence that lie beneath the surface, striving to connect with their higher selves and the universe at large. This pursuit not only enhances their personal growth but also enriches their relationships, as they bring depth and insight to their interactions with others.

In the context of spiritual growth, Life Path 7 individuals often find themselves drawn to practices that facilitate self-discovery and enlightenment. Meditation emerges as a powerful tool for introspection, allowing them to quiet the mind and tune into their inner wisdom. Through dedicated meditation techniques, they can cultivate mindfulness and clarity, enabling them to access deeper levels of consciousness. This practice not only aids in emotional regulation but also enhances their intuitive abilities, fostering a greater understanding of their life purpose and the interconnectedness of all beings.

Career paths for Life Path 7 individuals often reflect their desire for meaningful work. They are naturally inclined toward fields that allow for exploration, research, and creativity. Careers in psychology, counseling, spirituality, or the arts often resonate deeply with them. Finding a calling that aligns with their quest for meaning can lead to greater job satisfaction and fulfillment. By embracing their unique talents and interests, Life Path 7 individuals can create a professional life that not only supports their spiritual journey but also contributes positively to the world around them.

Relationships can be complex for those on Life Path 7, as their introspective nature may lead to periods of solitude and self-reflection. However, when they engage in meaningful connections, they bring depth and authenticity to their interactions. Understanding their emotional intelligence allows them to navigate relationships with empathy and insight. They often seek partners who can appreciate their need for space while also providing emotional support. Balancing their introversion with social engagement is essential, as it enables them to nurture fulfilling relationships that enhance their life journey.

Overcoming obstacles is an integral part of the Life Path 7 journey, as challenges often serve as catalysts for growth. By embracing these difficulties, individuals can unlock the wisdom hidden within their experiences. Cultivating resilience and a positive mindset empowers Life Path 7 individuals to face life's uncertainties with grace. As they continue to seek deeper meaning, they may discover that their challenges ultimately lead them to greater understanding and enlightenment, reinforcing their purpose as seekers of truth in a complex world.

Developing a Spiritual Practice

Developing a spiritual practice is essential for individuals on Life Path 7, as it aligns with their innate need for introspection and deeper understanding. Spirituality for Life Path 7 individuals often revolves around seeking truth and wisdom, making it vital to cultivate a practice that resonates with their unique qualities. Begin by establishing a routine that includes meditation, contemplation, or journaling, as these activities facilitate self-reflection and foster a connection to the inner self. The quiet moments spent in these practices allow Life Path 7 individuals to engage with their thoughts and feelings, offering clarity and insight into their spiritual journey.

Incorporating meditation techniques that resonate with Life Path 7 can significantly enhance spiritual growth. Practices such as mindfulness, guided meditations, or transcendental meditation can help in quieting the mind and creating a sacred space for exploration. Life Path 7 individuals may find that visualization techniques, focusing on their goals and dreams, can amplify their spiritual connections. Additionally, the use of crystals, essential oils, or sound healing can further deepen their meditative experience, allowing them to tap into higher realms of consciousness and understanding.

Creating a spiritual space at home can also support the development of a spiritual practice. This space should be a sanctuary where Life Path 7 individuals feel comfortable and inspired. Incorporating elements that reflect personal beliefs, such as meaningful symbols, serene colors, or nature-inspired decor, can make this space conducive to spiritual work. Regularly spending time in this space for meditation, reading spiritual texts, or engaging in creative expression can nurture their spiritual journey and provide a sense of peace and grounding.

As Life Path 7 individuals explore their spirituality, it is crucial to remain open to various teachings and philosophies. Engaging with different spiritual traditions, attending workshops, or reading literature on spirituality can broaden their understanding and provide valuable insights. This openness can lead to the discovery of practices that resonate deeply, contributing to their overall spiritual development. Embracing the journey of learning and growth, rather than seeking immediate answers, can help Life Path 7 individuals navigate their unique spiritual path with patience and curiosity.

Ultimately, developing a spiritual practice is about finding balance and authenticity in the search for enlightenment. Life Path 7 individuals should prioritize practices that align with their values and inner truths, allowing them to connect with their deeper selves and the universe. By integrating meditation, creating sacred spaces, and remaining open to new experiences, they can unlock the hidden gifts within themselves and embark on a fulfilling journey of spiritual enlightenment. This ongoing process of discovery not only enhances their personal growth but also enriches their relationships and enhances their emotional intelligence, paving the way for a more meaningful life.

Exploring Mystical and Esoteric Knowledge

Exploring the realms of mystical and esoteric knowledge is particularly significant for individuals on Life Path 7, who are naturally inclined toward introspection and deep understanding. Within the framework of numerology, Life Path 7 represents a journey of spiritual enlightenment, characterized by a quest for truth and wisdom. This quest often leads individuals to explore ancient teachings, mystical traditions, and esoteric practices that can illuminate their path. Engaging with these sources of knowledge not only enhances their spiritual growth but also helps them tap into their innate potential, encouraging the development of heightened intuition and emotional intelligence.

Life Path 7 individuals are often drawn to the metaphysical aspects of existence, seeking to uncover the hidden meanings behind life's experiences. This exploration can take many forms, including studying sacred texts, engaging in philosophical discourse, or practicing meditation and mindfulness. These practices serve as gateways to deeper understanding and connection with the universe. By immersing themselves in mystical traditions, such as Kabbalah or Hermeticism, Life Path 7 individuals can cultivate a sense of purpose and direction, aligning their personal journey with the broader tapestry of existence.

As they delve into esoteric knowledge, those on Life Path 7 may discover valuable insights into their careers and life callings. The rich symbolism and teachings found in mystical traditions can guide individuals toward paths that resonate with their spiritual essence. Whether through creative expression, healing practices, or other forms of service, embracing these insights can lead to fulfilling careers that align with their soul's purpose. Moreover, understanding the spiritual underpinnings of their work can enhance their emotional intelligence, enabling them to navigate relationships and professional dynamics with greater empathy and understanding.

Relationships play a crucial role in the journey of Life Path 7 individuals, and engaging with mystical knowledge can deepen their connections with others. By fostering a greater understanding of the energies and dynamics at play in their relationships, they can cultivate healthier and more harmonious interactions. The esoteric teachings often emphasize the importance of self-awareness and compassion, both of which are essential for navigating personal and professional relationships. By integrating these principles into their lives, Life Path 7 individuals can enhance their compatibility with others, creating meaningful bonds that support their spiritual growth.

Incorporating mystical and esoteric practices into daily life can also significantly impact health and wellness for Life Path 7 individuals. Techniques such as energy healing, chakra balancing, and mindful meditation can foster physical, emotional, and spiritual well-being. By prioritizing self-care and holistic practices, they can overcome obstacles and challenges that may arise on their path. Embracing these esoteric teachings not only nurtures their own growth but also empowers them to inspire others, illuminating the path to spiritual enlightenment for both themselves and those around them.

Chapter 4

Career and Life Path 7: Finding Your Calling

Identifying Suitable Careers

Identifying a suitable career is a crucial step for individuals on Life Path 7, as it aligns their innate gifts with the demands of the professional world. Life Path 7 individuals are often characterized by their analytical minds, deep intuition, and a strong inclination towards spirituality and introspection. These traits guide them toward careers that not only fulfill their intellectual curiosity but also resonate with their spiritual journey. It is essential for them to seek out roles that allow for solitude and reflection, as these environments foster their natural abilities and promote personal growth.

A key factor in identifying suitable careers for Life Path 7 individuals is understanding their unique strengths. Those on this path possess a profound ability to analyze situations, seek deeper meanings, and connect with others on an emotional level. Careers in research, psychology, or spiritual counseling can be particularly fulfilling. These roles provide opportunities to explore complex ideas and help others while allowing for the introspective time that Life Path 7 individuals crave. Additionally, creative outlets such as writing, art, or music can serve as powerful avenues for expression and self-discovery, enabling them to channel their inner thoughts and feelings.

Moreover, it is vital for Life Path 7 individuals to consider the work environment that best suits their temperament. Many thrive in settings that offer flexibility and autonomy, where they can work independently or in small groups. Remote work or freelance opportunities may be appealing, as they allow for a balance between professional responsibilities and personal reflection. Understanding the impact of social dynamics in the workplace can also guide them in making informed career choices that align with their introverted nature while still engaging with others when necessary.

Networking and mentorship can play a significant role in helping Life Path 7 individuals identify suitable careers. Engaging with like-minded people or seeking guidance from mentors who understand their spiritual journey can provide valuable insights into potential career paths. These connections can lead to opportunities that might not be readily apparent, allowing Life Path 7 individuals to navigate their career journey with confidence and clarity. It is important for them to remain open to new possibilities and experiences, as these often lead to profound personal and professional growth.

Lastly, maintaining a practice of self-reflection and meditation can greatly enhance the process of identifying a suitable career. Through meditation, Life Path 7 individuals can connect with their inner selves, gaining clarity on their passions and aspirations. This introspective practice allows them to better understand their true calling, aligning their career choices with their spiritual goals. Embracing their emotional intelligence and intuition will empower them to make decisions that resonate deeply, leading to a fulfilling career that supports their journey towards spiritual enlightenment.

Aligning Work with Spiritual Values

Aligning work with spiritual values is a transformative journey that resonates deeply with individuals on Life Path 7. This path is characterized by introspection, analytical thinking, and a quest for deeper truths. It is essential for those on this journey to recognize that their professional endeavors can serve as an extension of their spiritual beliefs. By ensuring that work aligns with spiritual values, individuals can create a harmonious balance between their inner selves and the external world, fostering a sense of fulfillment and purpose.

To begin, it is crucial for Life Path 7 individuals to identify their core spiritual values. These values often stem from personal beliefs, life experiences, and the quest for knowledge. Engaging in self-reflection, meditation, or journaling can aid in uncovering what truly matters. Once these values are identified, they can serve as a compass in making career decisions. For instance, if a Life Path 7 individual values authenticity and creativity, seeking out roles that allow for self-expression and innovation will lead to greater satisfaction and engagement in their work.

Moreover, the integration of spiritual practices into daily work life can enhance productivity and emotional well-being. Simple techniques such as mindfulness, meditation breaks, and positive affirmations can foster a work environment that nurtures spiritual growth. For instance, starting the day with a short meditation can help clear the mind and set intentions that align with one's spiritual values. This practice not only enhances focus but also creates a deeper connection to the work being undertaken, allowing Life Path 7 individuals to approach challenges with a calm and centered mindset.

Additionally, aligning work with spiritual values can strengthen relationships in the workplace. Life Path 7 individuals often thrive in environments where they can connect with like-minded individuals who share their values. By fostering open communication and mutual respect, they can create a supportive network that encourages both personal and professional growth. This sense of community not only enhances collaboration but also reinforces the importance of shared spiritual goals, ultimately contributing to a more positive and productive work atmosphere.

In conclusion, aligning work with spiritual values is a vital aspect of the Life Path 7 journey. As individuals seek to unlock their potential, they must remember that their career can be a powerful vehicle for spiritual expression. By identifying core values, integrating spiritual practices, and fostering meaningful relationships, Life Path 7 individuals can navigate their professional lives with purpose and clarity. This alignment not only leads to personal fulfillment but also contributes to a broader understanding of how spiritual growth and professional success can coexist harmoniously.

Overcoming Career Challenges

Overcoming career challenges is a crucial aspect of the journey for individuals on Life Path 7. These challenges often stem from their intrinsic nature, which values introspection, solitude, and deep understanding. Life Path 7 individuals may find themselves grappling with the demands of the external world, leading to feelings of disconnect or inadequacy in a fast-paced career environment. Recognizing that these challenges are not insurmountable is the first step towards unlocking their true potential. Embracing the unique strengths of Life Path 7 can transform these obstacles into opportunities for growth and fulfillment.

To effectively navigate career challenges, Life Path 7 individuals must harness their analytical skills and intuitive insights. These attributes enable them to assess situations deeply and identify underlying issues that may not be immediately apparent. By adopting a strategic approach to problem-solving, they can devise innovative solutions that align with their values and vision. This process requires patience and self-compassion, as the path to resolution may not always be linear. Engaging in self-reflection and journaling can facilitate clarity, allowing them to articulate their career aspirations and the barriers they face.

Networking and collaboration may initially feel daunting for those on Life Path 7, who often prefer solitude. However, building supportive relationships can significantly enhance their career trajectory. Seeking out mentors or like-minded individuals who understand their spiritual and intellectual pursuits can provide encouragement and guidance. As they learn to balance their need for introspection with social engagement, Life Path 7 individuals can create a network that nurtures their career ambitions while respecting their intrinsic nature. Establishing these connections is vital for personal growth and can lead to opportunities that resonate with their spiritual journey.

Mindfulness and meditation practices play a pivotal role in overcoming career challenges. These techniques help Life Path 7 individuals cultivate emotional intelligence, allowing them to manage stress and anxiety effectively. A regular meditation practice can enhance their focus and creativity, enabling them to approach challenges with a calm and centered mindset. By integrating mindfulness into their daily routines, they can develop resilience and adaptability, essential qualities for navigating the complexities of the professional world. This inner peace can serve as a foundation for making informed decisions that align with their purpose.

Ultimately, overcoming career challenges for Life Path 7 individuals involves a harmonious blend of introspection, connection, and self-care. By embracing their unique journey, they can transform obstacles into stepping stones towards their calling. Recognizing that every challenge is an opportunity for growth empowers them to pursue their passions fearlessly. As they navigate their careers with authenticity and purpose, they not only unlock their hidden gifts but also contribute to the collective spiritual evolution of those around them.

Chapter 5

Relationships and Compatibility for Life Path 7 Individuals

Understanding Relationship Dynamics

Understanding the dynamics of relationships is essential for individuals on Life Path 7, as these dynamics can significantly influence their spiritual journey and personal growth. Life Path 7 individuals, often characterized by introspection, analytical thinking, and a deep quest for truth, may find that their relationships are both a source of support and a challenge. The intricate balance between their need for solitude and the desire for connection is crucial to navigating the emotional landscape of their interactions with others. Recognizing these tendencies allows Life Path 7 individuals to cultivate healthier relationships that honor their unique needs while fostering deeper connections.

The emotional intelligence of Life Path 7 individuals plays a pivotal role in their relationships. Their natural inclination towards introspection often equips them with a profound understanding of their own emotions, but it also requires them to extend this awareness to others. Developing empathy and active listening skills can significantly enhance their ability to relate to partners, friends, and family members. By recognizing and validating the feelings of others, Life Path 7 individuals can build stronger bonds and create a nurturing environment that encourages open communication and mutual support.

Compatibility is another critical aspect of relationship dynamics for Life Path 7 individuals. While they may feel a strong connection to others who share similar spiritual or intellectual interests, they may also be drawn to partners who challenge their perspectives. Understanding the numerological compatibility with other Life Paths can provide valuable insights into potential strengths and challenges within these relationships. For instance, Life Path 3 and Life Path 5 may bring creativity and adventure to their lives, while Life Path 1 may offer leadership and ambition. Recognizing these patterns can help Life Path 7 individuals make informed choices in their romantic endeavors and friendships.

Navigating conflicts is an inevitable part of any relationship, and for Life Path 7 individuals, it often involves balancing their need for solitude with the demands of partnership. When faced with disagreements, they may retreat into their introspective nature, which can sometimes be misinterpreted as aloofness. To foster healthier conflict resolution, it is vital for Life Path 7 individuals to express their thoughts and feelings clearly while also being receptive to their partner's emotions. By engaging in open dialogue and practicing vulnerability, they can transform conflicts into opportunities for growth and understanding.

Ultimately, understanding relationship dynamics is a continual process for Life Path 7 individuals. As they evolve on their spiritual journey, they will encounter various relationships that reflect their growth, challenges, and aspirations. Embracing the lessons that each connection offers, whether it be through deep friendships or romantic partnerships, allows Life Path 7 individuals to unlock their potential in both personal and spiritual realms. By fostering self-awareness, emotional intelligence, and open communication, they can create fulfilling relationships that enrich their lives and support their path toward enlightenment.

Compatibility with Other Life Path Numbers

Compatibility among life path numbers is a vital consideration for those on the journey of self-discovery, particularly for individuals who resonate with the traits of life path 7. This number embodies introspection, spiritual seeking, and a quest for deeper truths. When examining compatibility, it is essential to understand that life path 7 individuals often thrive in relationships that respect their need for solitude and reflection, while also providing intellectual stimulation. The synergy between life path 7 and other numbers can significantly influence personal and relational growth, helping individuals unlock their potential while forging meaningful connections.

Life path 1 individuals, characterized by their leadership qualities and ambition, can create a dynamic partnership with life path 7. The proactive nature of life path 1 can encourage the often introspective 7 to take action, while the

7's reflective insights can help temper the 1's assertiveness. This combination can lead to a balanced relationship where both partners learn from each other's strengths, fostering personal growth and a shared journey toward success. However, it is crucial for both numbers to communicate openly about their needs, as life path 1's extroverted tendencies may sometimes overwhelm the more reserved 7.

In contrast, life path 2, known for their diplomatic and sensitive nature, often harmonizes beautifully with life path 7. The nurturing qualities of the 2 can provide a safe space for the 7 to express their deeper thoughts and feelings, allowing for a profound emotional connection. This partnership can flourish through mutual understanding and support, as both numbers value introspection and emotional depth. The gentle approach of life path 2 can help life path 7 navigate their emotional world, while the 7 can offer the 2 a broader perspective on life's mysteries, enriching their shared experiences.

Life path 3, with its creative and expressive energy, may present a different dynamic. While the outgoing 3 can inspire the 7 to engage more socially, the 7's contemplative nature might occasionally conflict with the 3's desire for constant interaction and fun. For this partnership to thrive, both individuals must find a balance between social engagement and the necessary quiet time that life path 7 craves. By respecting each other's differences and finding common ground in creativity and shared interests, they can cultivate a relationship that honors both partners' needs.

Lastly, life path 9, known for their humanitarianism and broad-minded approach, can resonate deeply with life path 7. Both numbers often seek deeper meaning in life, making their connection profound and spiritually enriching. The 9's compassionate nature complements the 7's introspection, allowing for deep conversations and shared ideals. However, both must remain aware of their tendencies to idealize and introspect, ensuring that they actively engage with the world around them. By embracing their unique qualities, life paths 7 and 9 can create an inspiring partnership, contributing positively to each other's personal and spiritual journeys.

Nurturing Healthy Relationships

Nurturing healthy relationships is essential for individuals on Life Path 7, as these connections serve as both a mirror and a catalyst for spiritual growth. Life Path 7 individuals often possess a deep yearning for knowledge and understanding, which can sometimes lead to emotional detachment. It is crucial for them to recognize that healthy relationships are not just about intellectual stimulation but also involve emotional intimacy and vulnerability. To cultivate such relationships, Life Path 7 individuals should focus on developing their emotional intelligence, allowing them to connect with others on a deeper level and foster bonds built on empathy and trust.

Active listening is a vital skill for nurturing relationships, especially for those on Life Path 7. While these individuals are naturally introspective, they must learn to engage fully in conversations. This includes not only hearing the words spoken but also understanding the feelings behind them. By

31

practicing active listening, Life Path 7 individuals can validate the experiences of others, making their loved ones feel valued and understood. Such engagement fosters a sense of belonging and strengthens the emotional ties that enrich their lives.

Setting healthy boundaries is another critical aspect of nurturing relationships for Life Path 7 individuals. Their introspective nature may lead them to retreat into solitude when overwhelmed, which can be misinterpreted by others as aloofness or disinterest. It is essential for Life Path 7 individuals to communicate their needs and boundaries openly. By doing so, they create a safe space for themselves and their loved ones, allowing for honest dialogue and mutual respect. This clarity can prevent misunderstandings and promote a more harmonious dynamic, paving the way for deeper connections.

Moreover, embracing shared experiences can significantly enhance the quality of relationships for Life Path 7 individuals. Engaging in activities that foster connection, whether through spiritual practices, creative pursuits, or social gatherings, allows for the emergence of meaningful interactions. Such experiences not only promote bonding but also provide Life Path 7 individuals with opportunities to express their unique perspectives and creativity. By inviting others into their world, they can cultivate a sense of community that resonates with their spiritual journey.

Lastly, it is vital for Life Path 7 individuals to engage in self-reflection and personal growth as part of nurturing their relationships. This journey inward allows them to identify patterns and areas for improvement in their interactions with others. By acknowledging their own vulnerabilities and working through personal challenges, they can approach relationships with a clearer mindset and an open heart. As they continue to evolve on their spiritual path, they can cultivate relationships that not only support their growth but also enrich the lives of those around them, fostering a cycle of mutual empowerment and love.

Chapter 6

Meditation Techniques for Life Path 7

The Importance of Meditation

Meditation holds a transformative power that resonates deeply with individuals on Life Path 7. This path is often characterized by introspection, a quest for knowledge, and a deep connection to the spiritual realm. For those navigating the complexities of Life Path 7, meditation serves as a vital practice to enhance self-awareness and foster a greater understanding of one's inner self. By regularly engaging in meditation, individuals can unlock the potential hidden within, cultivating a serene mind that is essential for personal growth and spiritual enlightenment.

For Life Path 7 individuals, who may often feel isolated in their quest for truth, meditation offers a sanctuary. It provides a space to retreat from the noise of the external world, allowing for deeper reflection and connection to one's intuition. This introspective nature of meditation aligns perfectly with the Life Path 7's innate tendencies, encouraging practitioners to explore their thoughts and emotions without judgment. As a result, meditation becomes a tool for emotional intelligence, enabling individuals to process their feelings and understand their reactions in relationships and other aspects of life.

In addition to fostering self-awareness, meditation enhances creativity and expression, critical components for those on Life Path 7. The stillness achieved during meditation can lead to moments of clarity and inspiration, allowing for the flow of creative ideas and solutions to emerge. By quieting the mind, Life Path 7 individuals can tap into their unique talents and gifts, which are often waiting to be discovered. This creative outlet not only enriches their personal lives but also plays a significant role in their career journeys, helping them find their calling and align their work with their spiritual values.

Moreover, meditation plays a crucial role in health and wellness practices for Life Path 7 individuals. The stress and anxiety that can accompany their introspective nature may lead to feelings of overwhelm. Regular meditation can act as a form of self-care, promoting relaxation and mental clarity. This practice encourages a holistic approach to well-being, where physical health, emotional balance, and spiritual growth coexist harmoniously. By incorporating meditation into their daily routines, Life Path 7 individuals can enhance their overall quality of life, allowing them to navigate challenges with greater resilience.

Finally, the importance of meditation extends to the balance between introversion and social engagement for those on Life Path 7. While these individuals often thrive in solitary pursuits, they also face the challenge of connecting with others. Meditation aids in developing a sense of inner peace that can translate into more meaningful interactions. As they strengthen their emotional intelligence through meditation, Life Path 7 individuals can engage in relationships with greater empathy and understanding. This balance enriches their lives, enabling them to form connections that support their spiritual journey while honoring their need for introspection.

Guided Meditations for Spiritual Growth

Guided meditations serve as a powerful tool for individuals on Life Path 7, providing a structured way to access inner wisdom and foster spiritual growth. These meditative practices are tailored to resonate with the unique characteristics of Life Path 7 individuals, who are often introspective, analytical, and spiritually inclined. By engaging in guided meditations, Life Path 7 seekers can deepen their understanding of themselves, explore their spiritual gifts, and cultivate a profound connection with the universe. This connection not only enhances personal growth but also aligns their actions with their life purpose.

One effective guided meditation focuses on the theme of self-discovery, allowing Life Path 7 individuals to explore their inner landscapes. Participants are encouraged to visualize their journey as they traverse through a serene forest, symbolizing the path to their highest self. As they encounter various elements of nature, such as flowing water and towering trees, they are guided to reflect on their life experiences, embracing both challenges and triumphs. This meditation nurtures emotional intelligence by inviting practitioners to acknowledge and process their feelings, ultimately leading to greater self-acceptance and understanding.

Another meditation technique emphasizes the importance of connecting with the divine. In this practice, Life Path 7 individuals are guided to visualize a radiant light surrounding them, symbolizing the presence of spiritual guides and higher consciousness. Through deep breathing and focused intention, participants can open their hearts and minds to receive messages and insights from the universe. This connection not only fosters spiritual growth but also enhances intuition, allowing Life Path 7 individuals to navigate their careers and relationships with greater clarity and purpose.

Additionally, guided meditations can address the challenges unique to Life Path 7, such as feelings of isolation or struggles with social engagement. A meditation designed to cultivate community and connection encourages participants to visualize themselves surrounded by supportive energies and like-minded individuals. This practice helps to overcome the natural inclination towards introversion, reinforcing the idea that connection and collaboration can be sources of strength. By embracing community through meditation, Life Path 7 individuals can enhance their emotional well-being and foster fulfilling relationships.

Finally, incorporating guided meditations into daily routines can significantly enhance overall health and wellness for those on Life Path 7. Meditative practices that focus on relaxation and stress reduction can help maintain balance amid the introspective nature of this life path. By dedicating time to mindfulness, Life Path 7 individuals can unlock their creative potential, allowing them to express themselves authentically in their careers and personal lives. Ultimately, guided meditations can serve as a transformative practice, empowering Life Path 7 individuals on their journey toward spiritual enlightenment and self-discovery.

Mindfulness Practices for Everyday Life

Mindfulness practices are essential tools for individuals on Life Path 7, as they foster a deeper connection with oneself and the universe. For those who are naturally introspective and often drawn to solitude, mindfulness offers a pathway to navigate the complexities of thoughts and emotions. Engaging in mindfulness helps Life Path 7 individuals cultivate awareness of the present moment, allowing them to transcend the distractions that often accompany their analytical and reflective tendencies. By incorporating mindfulness into daily life, individuals can uncover hidden gifts and insights that align with their spiritual journey.

One effective mindfulness practice is mindful breathing. Taking a few moments each day to focus solely on breathing can ground the mind and body. Life Path 7 individuals may find that their thoughts often race, leading to a sense of overwhelm. By directing attention to the breath, they can create a calming effect that anchors them in the present. This simple yet powerful practice not only alleviates stress but also enhances emotional intelligence, enabling a better understanding of one's feelings and reactions, which is crucial for personal growth.

Another beneficial practice is mindful walking. This involves engaging fully with the experience of walking, paying attention to the sensations in the feet, the rhythm of the breath, and the environment. For those on Life Path 7, who often wrestle with their inner world, mindful walking serves as a bridge to connect with nature and the external world. It encourages a sense of peace and clarity, facilitating spiritual growth and deeper insights into one's life path. By incorporating this practice into their routine, individuals can harmonize their introspective nature with the need for social engagement and connection.

Journaling is another powerful mindfulness tool for Life Path 7 individuals. Writing down thoughts, feelings, and experiences can help clarify complex emotions and thoughts. This practice allows for reflection and can reveal patterns or insights that may have otherwise gone unnoticed. By regularly engaging in journaling, individuals can track their spiritual journey, recognize their progress, and better understand their calling in career and relationships. This creative expression not only enriches their personal development but also opens doors to new opportunities aligned with their true self.

Lastly, incorporating mindfulness into daily activities, such as eating or even washing dishes, encourages a state of presence. By focusing on the textures, flavors, and sensations, Life Path 7 individuals can transform mundane tasks into opportunities for spiritual connection. This practice cultivates gratitude and appreciation for the simple joys of life, supporting overall wellness and emotional balance. Through consistent mindfulness practices, those on Life Path 7 can unlock their hidden gifts, navigating their journey with greater clarity, purpose, and fulfillment.

Chapter 7

Life Path 7 and Emotional Intelligence

Understanding Emotional Intelligence

Emotional intelligence is a vital skill that can significantly enhance the journey of individuals on Life Path 7. This path, often characterized by introspection, spiritual seeking, and analytical thinking, requires a nuanced understanding of one's emotions and the emotions of others. Life Path 7 individuals typically thrive in solitary environments where they can explore their inner worlds, yet developing emotional intelligence allows them to navigate social interactions more effectively. By honing this skill, they can deepen their relationships, enhance their spiritual growth, and ultimately align their emotional awareness with their intellectual pursuits.

At its core, emotional intelligence comprises several key components: self-awareness, self-regulation, social awareness, and relationship management. For Life Path 7 individuals, cultivating self-awareness is particularly crucial, as it enables them to recognize their emotional triggers and understand how these feelings influence their thoughts and behaviors. This self-understanding not only fosters personal growth but also cultivates a deeper connection with one's spiritual path. Engaging in practices such as meditation can enhance self-awareness, providing a space for reflection and emotional clarity.

Self-regulation, another essential component of emotional intelligence, allows Life Path 7 individuals to manage their emotional responses effectively. Given their propensity for introspection, they may sometimes struggle with anxiety or self-doubt. Learning to regulate these emotions through techniques such as mindfulness can empower them to respond to challenges with composure rather than reactivity. By mastering self-regulation, they can transform potential obstacles into opportunities for growth, enhancing their resilience on both personal and spiritual levels.

Social awareness and relationship management are equally important for those on Life Path 7. As these individuals often prefer solitude, developing the ability to empathize with others and navigate social situations can be challenging yet rewarding. By actively listening to others and being attuned to non-verbal cues, Life Path 7 individuals can foster deeper connections and enrich their relationships. This emotional insight complements their analytical skills, creating a unique balance that enables them to communicate their ideas and feelings more effectively while also appreciating the perspectives of others.

In conclusion, understanding emotional intelligence is a transformative aspect of the Life Path 7 experience. By cultivating self-awareness, self-regulation, social awareness, and relationship management, individuals on this path can unlock their potential for spiritual growth, enhance their interpersonal relationships, and find fulfillment in their personal and professional lives. As they learn to navigate the complexities of their emotions and those of others, they will discover that emotional intelligence is not just a skill but a key to unlocking the hidden gifts that life has to offer.

Developing Self-Awareness

Developing self-awareness is a crucial aspect of the journey for individuals on Life Path 7. This path is characterized by introspection, analysis, and a quest for deeper understanding. As seekers of truth, Life Path 7 individuals often find themselves drawn to explore their inner worlds and the mysteries of existence. To harness the full potential of this path, developing self-awareness is essential. It not only facilitates personal growth but also enhances one's ability to connect with others and navigate life's challenges effectively.

To begin cultivating self-awareness, Life Path 7 individuals should engage in reflective practices that encourage introspection. Journaling is a powerful tool for this purpose, allowing individuals to articulate their thoughts, feelings, and experiences. By writing down daily reflections, one can identify patterns in behavior and thought processes, gaining insights into their motivations and desires. This practice can reveal the underlying beliefs that shape one's identity and influence relationships, providing a clearer picture of the self and paving the way for personal transformation.

Meditation is another effective technique for developing self-awareness. Life Path 7 individuals often resonate with the contemplative nature of meditation, which promotes inner stillness and clarity. Through regular practice, one can learn to observe thoughts without judgment, fostering a deeper understanding of emotional responses and habitual reactions. This heightened awareness can lead to increased emotional intelligence, enabling individuals to manage their feelings more effectively and respond to life's challenges with a calm and centered mindset. As they cultivate this inner awareness, Life Path 7 individuals may find themselves better equipped to navigate their spiritual journeys.

Engaging with the natural world can also enhance self-awareness for those on Life Path 7. Nature has a unique ability to ground individuals, providing a space for reflection and connection. Spending time outdoors, whether through hiking, gardening, or simply observing the environment, encourages a sense of peace and clarity. This connection to nature can stimulate profound realizations about one's place in the universe and inspire creative expression. By immersing themselves in natural surroundings, Life Path 7 individuals can gain insights that deepen their understanding of themselves and their spiritual paths.

Lastly, seeking feedback from trusted friends or mentors can further support the development of self-awareness. Life Path 7 individuals may sometimes struggle with self-perception, leading to blind spots in their understanding of themselves. By inviting constructive criticism and reflections from others, individuals can gain new perspectives on their strengths and areas for growth. This external feedback, combined with inner exploration, creates a holistic approach to self-awareness, allowing Life Path 7 individuals to embrace their unique gifts while addressing the challenges they face. Ultimately, developing self-awareness is a foundational step in unlocking the hidden gifts of Life Path 7, guiding individuals toward spiritual enlightenment and fulfillment.

Enhancing Empathy and Social Skills

Empathy and social skills are essential components of personal development, particularly for individuals on Life Path 7. While Life Path 7 individuals often possess deep introspective qualities and analytical minds, enhancing their empathy can bridge the gap between their inner world and external relationships. Empathy allows Life Path 7s to connect with others on a more profound level, enriching their interpersonal experiences and fostering a sense of community. By recognizing and validating the emotions of others, Life Path 7s can cultivate deeper relationships that resonate with their spiritual journey.

To enhance empathy, Life Path 7 individuals can engage in active listening practices. This involves not just hearing words but truly understanding the feelings and intentions behind them. Practicing mindfulness during conversations allows Life Path 7s to stay present and attuned to the emotional states of those around them. This heightened awareness can lead to more meaningful interactions, as individuals learn to respond with compassion rather than mere intellectual analysis. Journaling about daily interactions can also help Life Path 7s reflect on their emotional responses and consider how they might better connect with others in the future.

Social skills, often viewed as a more extroverted trait, can also be developed through intentional practice. Life Path 7 individuals may find social situations to be draining, yet participating in group activities can provide valuable opportunities for growth. Joining clubs or pursuing community activities that align with their interests can help them practice social engagement in a comfortable setting. Moreover, setting small, achievable goals for social interactions—such as initiating a conversation or expressing appreciation—can build confidence and enhance overall social competence.

Incorporating meditation techniques focused on compassion can further support the development of empathy and social skills. Guided meditations that emphasize loving-kindness can help Life Path 7s extend their understanding and compassion toward others. By visualizing others' challenges and sending them positive intentions, they can foster a sense of connection that transcends their natural inclination toward introspection. This practice not only enhances empathy but also contributes to emotional intelligence, allowing Life Path 7s to respond to social situations with greater emotional awareness.

Ultimately, enhancing empathy and social skills is a vital aspect of the spiritual growth journey for Life Path 7 individuals. By embracing opportunities for connection and reflection, they can transform their relationships and enrich their lives. This process not only fosters personal fulfillment but also aligns with their higher purpose of understanding the deeper truths of life. As they navigate their journey, developing these skills will empower Life Path 7s to unlock their potential and contribute positively to the world around them.

Chapter 8

Health and Wellness Practices for Life Path 7

Holistic Approaches to Health

Holistic approaches to health emphasize the interconnectedness of the mind, body, and spirit, aligning seamlessly with the innate characteristics of Life Path 7 individuals. This path often embodies introspection and a quest for deeper understanding, making it crucial for those on this journey to recognize the importance of balancing physical health with mental and spiritual well-being. By embracing a holistic perspective, Life Path 7 individuals can unlock their full potential and cultivate a lifestyle that supports their unique gifts and spiritual aspirations.

Nutrition serves as a foundational aspect of holistic health, and for Life Path 7 individuals, the choice of food can significantly impact cognitive clarity and emotional stability. A diet rich in whole foods, such as fruits, vegetables, whole grains, and lean proteins, nourishes not only the body but also the mind, enhancing the intellectual pursuits that Life Path 7 individuals often engage in. Mindful eating practices, such as being present during meals and appreciating the nourishment they provide, can further deepen the connection between food and overall wellness. This approach encourages a reflective mindset, allowing for greater awareness of how different foods affect mood and energy levels.

Physical activity is another critical element of a holistic health regimen. Life Path 7 individuals may find themselves drawn to activities that allow for solitary reflection, such as yoga or hiking, which promote physical fitness while also nurturing the spirit. Incorporating regular movement into daily routines not only enhances physical health but also supports mental clarity and emotional resilience. Engaging in outdoor activities can foster a connection with nature, which is especially beneficial for those who thrive on introspection and solitude. This balance of physical exertion and spiritual grounding creates a harmonious environment for personal growth.

Mental and emotional health practices are vital components of a holistic approach. Life Path 7 individuals often possess a rich inner world, making it essential to cultivate emotional intelligence and resilience. Techniques such as meditation, journaling, and mindfulness can provide valuable tools for processing emotions and fostering self-awareness. These practices encourage Life Path 7 individuals to explore their feelings deeply, leading to greater understanding and acceptance of their emotional landscape. Additionally, establishing supportive relationships with like-minded individuals can enhance emotional well-being and provide a nurturing space for sharing insights and experiences.

Finally, integrating spiritual practices into daily life can profoundly influence overall health and wellness for Life Path 7 individuals. Engaging in activities such as prayer, meditation, or energy healing can help align the spirit with the physical and mental aspects of existence. These practices not only foster a sense of connection to the universe but also enhance personal insight and clarity. By weaving spirituality into the fabric of everyday life, those on the Life Path 7 journey can unlock deeper layers of understanding, cultivating a holistic approach that nurtures their unique gifts and supports their quest for enlightenment.

Nutrition and its Impact on Spiritual Well-being

Nutrition plays a critical role in shaping not only physical health but also spiritual well-being, especially for individuals on Life Path 7. This path often emphasizes introspection, analytical thinking, and a deep connection to the metaphysical. The foods we consume can significantly influence our mental clarity, emotional stability, and overall energy levels, which in turn affects our spiritual practices and growth. A balanced diet that nourishes the body can enhance the mind's ability to connect with spiritual insights and wisdom, allowing Life Path 7 individuals to explore their spiritual journey more profoundly.

Incorporating whole, nutrient-dense foods into daily routines can foster a clearer mind and a more attuned spirit. Foods rich in omega-3 fatty acids, such as fish, walnuts, and flaxseeds, support brain health and cognitive function. This is particularly beneficial for Life Path 7 individuals, who often seek deeper understanding and knowledge. Additionally, fruits and vegetables packed with vitamins and antioxidants can help to cleanse the body of toxins, promoting a sense of lightness and clarity that is essential for meditation and spiritual reflection. By prioritizing such foods, Life Path 7 individuals can cultivate an environment conducive to spiritual practice.

Hydration is another crucial aspect of nutrition that cannot be overlooked. Water is essential for maintaining optimal brain function and emotional balance. For those on a spiritual journey, staying adequately hydrated can facilitate deeper meditation experiences and enhance intuitive abilities. Herbal teas, such as chamomile or peppermint, can also provide calming effects, helping to ground Life Path 7 individuals during their contemplative practices. Emphasizing the importance of hydration can lead to a more vibrant spiritual life, allowing for clearer insights and a stronger connection to one's inner self.

Moreover, the practice of mindful eating can significantly enhance the spiritual journey of Life Path 7 individuals. This involves being present during meals, appreciating the flavors and textures, and acknowledging the nourishment being provided. Mindful eating encourages a deeper connection to the body and its needs, fostering self-awareness and promoting emotional intelligence. By recognizing the impact of food on their spiritual well-being, Life Path 7 individuals can make more conscious choices that align with their spiritual goals and personal development.

Lastly, it is essential to consider the role of food choices in building harmonious relationships. The energy we bring into our interactions can be influenced by our diet and overall health. By choosing nourishing foods, Life Path 7 individuals can elevate their vibrational frequency, making them more open and receptive in their relationships. This heightened sense of well-being and clarity can lead to more meaningful connections, further enhancing the spiritual journey. In this way, nutrition becomes a vital tool for Life Path 7 individuals, helping them unlock their potential and navigate their unique path toward spiritual enlightenment.

Physical Activities for Balance

Physical activities play a crucial role in fostering balance, particularly for individuals on the Life Path 7, who often navigate the complexities of introspection and spiritual exploration. Engaging in physical activities that promote balance not only enhances physical well-being but also supports mental clarity and emotional stability. Activities such as yoga, tai chi, and Pilates are excellent choices for Life Path 7 individuals, as they encourage a harmonious connection between the body and mind. These practices cultivate mindfulness, allowing practitioners to align their physical movements with their inner thoughts and feelings, creating a holistic sense of balance.

Yoga, in particular, offers a variety of poses that enhance physical stability while promoting spiritual growth. Life Path 7 individuals may find solace in the meditative aspects of yoga, where each pose serves as an opportunity for self-reflection and connection to the present moment. The practice of breath control, or pranayama, within yoga not only strengthens the body but also calms the mind, facilitating deeper introspection. As Life Path 7 individuals explore different yoga styles, they can choose practices that resonate with their unique spiritual journey, enabling them to unlock deeper layers of their potential.

Tai chi, often described as "meditation in motion," provides another excellent avenue for Life Path 7 individuals to achieve balance. The slow, deliberate movements encourage a state of mindfulness that is essential for spiritual growth. As practitioners learn to flow gracefully from one posture to another, they develop greater body awareness and coordination, which can translate into improved emotional intelligence. This heightened awareness allows Life Path 7 individuals to navigate their relationships more effectively, enhancing compatibility and understanding with others.

Pilates, focusing on core strength and stability, offers a different but equally valuable approach to physical activity. This method emphasizes control and precision, which can be particularly beneficial for introspective individuals seeking to ground themselves in their physicality. By strengthening the core, Life Path 7 individuals can experience improved posture and alignment, both physically and metaphorically. This newfound strength provides the confidence needed to tackle life's challenges, empowering them to pursue their calling while maintaining emotional equilibrium.

Incorporating a variety of physical activities into a balanced routine can significantly impact the overall well-being of Life Path 7 individuals. These practices not only enhance physical health but also support their spiritual journey by fostering a deeper connection with their inner selves. As they explore yoga, tai chi, and Pilates, Life Path 7 individuals can discover new dimensions of personal growth, emotional intelligence, and creative expression. Ultimately, these physical activities serve as powerful tools in unlocking the hidden gifts of Life Path 7, paving the way for a fulfilling and balanced life.

Chapter 9

Creativity and Expression in Life Path 7

The Role of Creativity in Spiritual Growth

Creativity serves as a vital conduit for spiritual growth, especially for individuals on the Life Path 7. This path is characterized by introspection, deep thinking, and a quest for truth, all of which can be greatly enhanced through creative expression. Engaging in creative pursuits allows Life Path 7 individuals to tap into their inner selves, facilitating a deeper understanding of their thoughts, emotions, and spiritual aspirations. Whether through writing, art, music, or other forms of expression, creativity becomes a tool for exploration and discovery, helping to unlock the hidden aspects of their personality and spiritual journey.

The process of creation often mirrors the journey of spiritual enlightenment. Life Path 7 individuals thrive in environments that encourage reflection and contemplation. By channeling their thoughts and feelings into creative projects, they can navigate their spiritual landscapes more effectively. This process not only provides a means of self-discovery but also fosters a sense of connection with the universe. As they create, they begin to recognize patterns and insights that resonate with their spiritual beliefs, enhancing their understanding of their life's purpose.

Moreover, creativity can serve as a bridge between the intellectual and the spiritual realms for Life Path 7 individuals. Many on this path possess a strong analytical mind, often leading them to seek logical explanations for the mysteries of life. However, creativity allows them to step beyond the confines of rational thinking, inviting intuition and inspiration into their lives. This balance between intellect and intuition is crucial for spiritual growth, as it enables Life Path 7 individuals to embrace the unknown and cultivate a deeper connection with their spiritual essence.

In addition to personal exploration, creative expression can also strengthen relationships. Life Path 7 individuals may sometimes struggle with social engagement due to their introspective nature. By sharing their creative endeavors with others, they can foster connections that resonate on a deeper level. Whether through collaborative projects or simply sharing their work, creativity can act as a catalyst for meaningful conversations and relationships. This not only nurtures their emotional intelligence but also enhances their social interactions, creating a harmonious balance between their inner world and the outside community.

Ultimately, embracing creativity is essential for Life Path 7 individuals seeking spiritual growth. By engaging in creative practices, they can explore their spiritual beliefs, develop a deeper understanding of themselves, and foster meaningful connections with others. This journey through creativity not only enriches their personal lives but also contributes to their overall well-being and enlightenment. As they unlock their creative potential, Life Path 7 individuals pave the way for a more fulfilling and spiritually aligned existence.

Finding Your Creative Outlet

Finding a creative outlet is a vital aspect of the journey for individuals on Life Path 7. This path emphasizes introspection, analytical thinking, and a thirst for knowledge, often leading to a rich inner world. However, the challenge lies in translating this depth of thought and feeling into creative expression. Engaging in creative activities not only serves as a means of self-discovery but also fosters emotional intelligence, allowing Life Path 7 individuals to connect with their innermost selves and the world around them.

To identify a suitable creative outlet, it is essential for Life Path 7 individuals to explore various forms of expression. This may include writing, painting, music, or even more unconventional methods like dance or digital art. The key is to experiment without judgment, giving oneself permission to explore different mediums. As analytical thinkers, Life Path 7 individuals may initially approach creativity with a sense of skepticism; however, embracing spontaneity can lead to profound revelations about their true passions and gifts.

Meditation plays a significant role in enhancing creativity for those on Life Path 7. By quieting the mind and allowing thoughts to flow freely, individuals can tap into their subconscious, where innovative ideas often reside. Regular meditation not only improves focus but also fosters an environment conducive to creative thoughts. Incorporating visualization techniques during meditation can help Life Path 7 individuals envision their creative pursuits, providing clarity on the direction they wish to take.

Collaborating with others can also be a powerful way to find a creative outlet. Life Path 7 individuals may find themselves feeling isolated due to their introspective nature; however, engaging with like-minded individuals can spark new ideas and provide encouragement. Joining workshops, attending art classes, or participating in community events can create opportunities for collaboration and inspiration, reinforcing the notion that creativity often flourishes in a supportive environment.

Ultimately, the journey of finding a creative outlet is deeply personal for those on Life Path 7. It is essential to approach this exploration with an open heart and mind, allowing for growth and transformation. As they delve into their creative pursuits, Life Path 7 individuals will not only enhance their spiritual growth but also enrich their lives and the lives of those around them. By unlocking their creative potential, they embrace a vital aspect of their existence, paving the way for a more fulfilling and harmonious life journey.

Expressing Your Unique Voice

Expressing your unique voice is an essential aspect of the journey for individuals on Life Path 7. As seekers of truth, these individuals often find themselves delving deep into their inner worlds, exploring their thoughts, emotions, and spiritual beliefs. This introspection is a powerful tool for self-discovery, allowing Life Path 7 individuals to articulate their unique perspectives and insights. By understanding how to express themselves authentically, they can contribute meaningfully to the world around them, fostering deeper connections in both personal and professional spheres.

One of the cornerstones of expressing your unique voice lies in embracing vulnerability. Life Path 7 individuals often grapple with feelings of isolation or the pressure to conform to societal expectations. By allowing themselves to be vulnerable, they create an authentic space for their voice to emerge. This process involves sharing their thoughts and feelings honestly, whether through written expression, art, or verbal communication. Such authentic expression not only enriches their own lives but also resonates with others who may feel similarly, fostering a sense of community and understanding.

In the realm of creativity, Life Path 7 individuals often possess an innate artistic flair, whether through writing, music, or visual arts. Engaging in creative pursuits is a powerful way to channel their unique voice. It is essential for them to explore various forms of expression, allowing themselves the freedom to experiment without the confines of perfectionism. This exploration can lead to profound insights and innovations, as creativity often serves as a bridge between the mind's deeper explorations and the external world. By embracing their creative instincts, Life Path 7 individuals can discover new dimensions of themselves and share these revelations with others.

Meditation and mindfulness practices also play a crucial role in helping Life Path 7 individuals express their unique voice. These practices encourage self-reflection and clarity, allowing individuals to connect with their inner selves and understand their core beliefs and values. By dedicating time to stillness and introspection, they can cultivate a deeper understanding of their thoughts and feelings, which can then be articulated through various means of expression. This alignment between inner awareness and outward expression fosters authenticity, enabling them to communicate their truth more effectively.

Lastly, the journey of expressing one's unique voice is intertwined with the broader themes of spiritual growth and emotional intelligence. Life Path 7 individuals are often drawn to spiritual practices that enhance their understanding of themselves and their connection to the universe. By integrating these insights into their expressions, they not only articulate their personal experiences but also contribute to the collective understanding of spiritual concepts. Developing emotional intelligence further enriches this journey, as it allows them to navigate complex interpersonal dynamics, fostering deeper relationships and enhancing their ability to communicate effectively. Through these combined efforts, Life Path 7 individuals can unlock their potential, sharing their unique voice with the world and inspiring others on their own journeys.

Chapter 10

Life Path 7 Challenges and Overcoming Obstacles

Common Challenges Faced by Life Path 7 Individuals

Life Path 7 individuals often find themselves navigating a unique set of challenges that can significantly impact their spiritual and personal development. One of the most common difficulties faced by those on this path is their tendency towards introspection and isolation. While the reflective nature of Life Path 7 allows for deep insights and understanding, it can also lead to feelings of loneliness and disconnection from the world. This introspective nature may create a barrier to forming meaningful relationships, as they may struggle to open up to others or find it challenging to relate to those who do not share their depth of thought and spiritual curiosity.

Another significant challenge is the pursuit of knowledge and truth, which can lead to frustration when faced with the complexities of life. Life Path 7 individuals often possess a strong desire to seek answers, but the quest for understanding can become overwhelming, particularly when confronted with ambiguous situations or conflicting information. This relentless search for truth can result in periods of anxiety and self-doubt, as they grapple with existential questions that may not have clear answers. Developing patience and accepting that some questions may remain unanswered is crucial for their emotional and spiritual growth.

Career choices can also pose a challenge for Life Path 7 individuals, who may feel drawn to unconventional paths or careers that allow for intellectual exploration and creativity. However, the pressure to conform to societal expectations can create internal conflict. Those on this path may struggle to find a career that aligns with their values and allows for spiritual growth, often feeling unfulfilled in traditional roles. It's essential for Life Path 7 individuals to seek careers that resonate with their inner calling, embracing opportunities that nurture their intellectual and spiritual needs while providing a sense of purpose.

In relationships, Life Path 7 individuals may encounter difficulties due to their inherent need for solitude and introspection. Partners may find it challenging to understand their need for space, which can lead to misunderstandings and feelings of neglect. Additionally, the intense focus on personal development can sometimes overshadow the importance of nurturing relationships. To foster healthy connections, Life Path 7 individuals must work on balancing their need for independence with the need for companionship, ensuring that they communicate openly with their partners about their emotional needs.

Lastly, emotional intelligence can be a double-edged sword for Life Path 7 individuals. While they possess a heightened awareness of their own emotions and the emotions of others, this sensitivity can lead to emotional overwhelm. They may find themselves absorbing the feelings of those around them, resulting in emotional fatigue. Developing effective coping strategies, such as meditation and mindfulness practices, is essential for managing this emotional intensity. By learning to establish healthy boundaries and prioritize self-care, Life Path 7 individuals can navigate their challenges with greater ease, ultimately leading to a more balanced and fulfilling life journey.

Strategies for Resilience

Resilience is a vital quality for individuals on Life Path 7, as it enables them to navigate the complexities of their spiritual journey while remaining grounded in their unique gifts. To cultivate resilience, it is essential for Life Path 7 individuals to embrace their introspective nature. This means taking the time to reflect on personal experiences, acknowledging emotions, and understanding the lessons inherent in challenges. Journaling can be an effective tool in this regard, allowing for deeper self-exploration and the identification of patterns that may hinder growth. By recognizing these patterns, Life Path 7 individuals can develop strategies to overcome obstacles and emerge stronger.

Another key strategy for building resilience lies in the practice of mindfulness and meditation. Life Path 7 individuals often possess a profound connection to the spiritual realm, and enhancing this connection through meditation can foster inner strength and clarity. Mindfulness techniques, such as focused breathing and visualization, help to create mental space, enabling individuals to confront difficulties with a calm and centered mindset. Regular meditation not only promotes emotional intelligence but also empowers Life Path 7 individuals to respond to life's challenges with grace and confidence.

Social connections are vital for fostering resilience, even for the more introverted Life Path 7 individuals. Building a supportive network can provide encouragement and strength during trying times. Engaging in meaningful relationships, whether through close friendships or community involvement, allows Life Path 7 individuals to share their experiences and gain insights from others. These connections can also serve as a reminder of shared humanity, reinforcing the idea that challenges are part of the collective journey. Finding balance in social engagement—participating in group activities while also honoring the need for solitude—can further enhance resilience.

Incorporating physical health practices into daily routines is another essential strategy for resilience. Life Path 7 individuals often thrive when they prioritize holistic wellness, recognizing the mind-body connection. Regular exercise, a balanced diet, and adequate rest can significantly influence emotional well-being and resilience. Activities such as yoga or tai chi not only promote physical health but also cultivate a sense of inner peace, helping to manage stress and anxiety. By adopting healthy lifestyle habits, Life Path 7 individuals can build a strong foundation that supports their spiritual and emotional journeys.

Lastly, embracing creativity and self-expression plays a crucial role in enhancing resilience for Life Path 7 individuals. Engaging in creative pursuits, whether through art, writing, or music, allows for the exploration of emotions and thoughts that may be difficult to articulate otherwise. This form of expression serves as an outlet for processing experiences and can lead to profound insights and healing. Encouraging creativity fosters a sense of accomplishment and joy, reinforcing the idea that even amidst challenges, there exists an opportunity for growth and transformation. By integrating these strategies into their lives, Life Path 7 individuals can unlock their potential and navigate their spiritual journey with resilience and confidence.

Transforming Challenges into Opportunities

Transforming challenges into opportunities is a pivotal aspect of the journey for individuals on Life Path 7. This path, characterized by introspection, analytical thinking, and a quest for spiritual truth, often presents unique hurdles that may initially appear daunting. However, these challenges can serve as powerful catalysts for personal growth and enlightenment. Embracing the trials of Life Path 7 allows individuals to tap into their hidden gifts and develop a deeper understanding of themselves and the world around them.

For Life Path 7 individuals, challenges often manifest in the form of self-doubt, existential questions, and the struggle for connection. These experiences can lead to feelings of isolation, but they also provide an opportunity for profound self-discovery. By reframing these obstacles as stepping stones rather than barriers, Life Path 7 individuals can cultivate resilience. This shift in perspective not only enhances emotional intelligence but also fosters a deeper connection to one's life purpose, ultimately guiding them toward their true calling.

In the realm of career and professional growth, the ability to transform challenges into opportunities is crucial for Life Path 7 individuals. Many find themselves drawn to fields that require deep analytical skills and a touch of creativity, such as research, psychology, or the arts. When faced with setbacks, such as job dissatisfaction or career stagnation, those on this path can use these experiences to reassess their goals, explore new avenues, and align their professional lives more closely with their spiritual aspirations. This proactive approach can lead to fulfilling careers that resonate with their inner selves.

Relationships, too, can present challenges for Life Path 7 individuals, particularly due to their introspective nature. The tendency to seek solitude can create misunderstandings with partners or friends. However, viewing these challenges as opportunities for growth can lead to more authentic connections. By engaging in open communication and expressing their needs, Life Path 7 individuals can deepen their relationships. This process not only strengthens bonds but also enhances their emotional intelligence, allowing them to navigate interpersonal dynamics with greater ease and empathy.

Finally, embracing mindfulness and meditation techniques can significantly aid Life Path 7 individuals in transforming challenges into opportunities. These practices offer a space for reflection and clarity, enabling them to process their experiences and insights effectively. By integrating mindfulness into their daily routines, they can develop a greater awareness of their thoughts and emotions, thus transforming negative patterns into opportunities for healing and growth. This holistic approach not only nurtures mental well-being but also aligns with their spiritual journey, facilitating a deeper connection to their inner wisdom and the universe.

Chapter 11

Numerology and Personal Development for Life Path 7

The Basics of Numerology

Numerology is an ancient metaphysical science that explores the significance of numbers and their influence on our lives. At its core, numerology is based on the belief that numbers carry vibrational frequencies that can provide insights into our personalities, life paths, and destinies. For individuals on Life Path 7, understanding the basics of numerology is essential to unlocking their potential and harnessing the unique traits that define their spiritual journey. This subchapter will delve into the foundational elements of numerology, offering Life Path 7 individuals and numerologists a framework for deeper exploration.

The primary components of numerology include life path numbers, expression numbers, soul urge numbers, and personality numbers. The life path number, derived from one's date of birth, is the most significant in determining an individual's journey and purpose. For Life Path 7 individuals, this number symbolizes introspection, analysis, and a quest for truth. By understanding the attributes associated with

Life Path 7, such as a deep yearning for knowledge and a tendency toward solitude, individuals can navigate their spiritual growth more effectively.

In addition to the life path number, expression and soul urge numbers complement the understanding of one's spiritual makeup. The expression number, calculated from the full birth name, reveals the talents and skills one is meant to develop. For Life Path 7 individuals, this number may highlight abilities related to research, communication, and teaching. Meanwhile, the soul urge number, derived from the vowels in the name, reflects the inner motivations and desires that drive an individual. By examining these additional numbers, Life Path 7 individuals can gain a more comprehensive view of their personal development and emotional intelligence.

Numerology also emphasizes the significance of the master numbers 11, 22, and 33, which carry heightened spiritual meaning. While these numbers might not directly correspond to Life Path 7, understanding their implications can enrich one's perspective on spiritual growth and the challenges faced along the journey. Life Path 7 individuals can learn valuable lessons from these master numbers, particularly in areas such as intuition, leadership, and service to others. Recognizing how these energies interact with their own can lead to profound insights and a more balanced approach to life.

Ultimately, the basics of numerology provide Life Path 7 individuals with a powerful tool for self-discovery and personal transformation. By integrating numerological insights into their daily lives, they can cultivate a deeper understanding of their purpose, enhance their relationships, and align their career paths with their spiritual calling. This knowledge not only aids in overcoming obstacles but also fosters creativity and expression, allowing Life Path 7 individuals to thrive in their unique journey toward enlightenment.

Using Numerology for Self-Discovery

Numerology serves as a profound tool for self-discovery, particularly for individuals on Life Path 7, who are often introspective and spiritually inclined. By examining the significant numbers associated with one's birth date and name, Life Path 7 individuals can unveil deeper insights into their personality, strengths, and challenges. This practice encourages personal reflection and helps individuals understand their innate tendencies, allowing them to align their actions with their true selves. The numerical vibrations can illuminate the path toward spiritual growth, offering guidance in areas such as career choices, relationships, and personal development.

A key aspect of using numerology for self-discovery involves analyzing the Life Path number itself, which signifies the overarching themes and lessons in one's life. For Life Path 7 individuals, this number often resonates with wisdom, analytical thinking, and a quest for truth. By understanding these traits, they can harness their natural abilities to seek knowledge and engage in meaningful pursuits. This self-awareness can lead to fulfilling career paths, as Life Path 7 people often thrive in roles that allow for independent exploration, research, or spiritual guidance.

In addition to the Life Path number, exploring personal year cycles can enhance the self-discovery process. Each year brings a unique vibration that influences experiences and opportunities. Life Path 7 individuals can benefit from understanding these cycles to navigate their personal and professional lives more effectively. For instance, a year focused on partnerships may encourage them to strengthen relationships, while a year of introspection might be ideal for deepening spiritual practices or creative endeavors. Recognizing these cycles fosters a greater sense of empowerment and adaptability.

Meditation techniques can also be integrated into the exploration of numerology for self-discovery. These practices enable Life Path 7 individuals to connect with their inner selves and reflect on the insights gained through numerological analysis. Meditation can facilitate clarity and enhance emotional intelligence, allowing them to process their thoughts and feelings more deeply. By incorporating numerology into their meditative practices, they can visualize their numbers and affirm their personal truths, leading to transformative insights and a deeper understanding of their life's purpose.

Ultimately, using numerology for self-discovery empowers Life Path 7 individuals to embrace their unique journey. By recognizing their strengths and acknowledging their challenges, they can cultivate a balanced approach to life that honors their introverted nature while engaging with the world meaningfully. This self-awareness not only aids in personal development but also enhances relationships, career satisfaction, and overall well-being. As they unlock the hidden gifts within their Life Path, they embark on a journey toward spiritual enlightenment and fulfillment.

Life Path 7 in the Context of Personal Development

Life Path 7 individuals are often characterized by their deep introspection and analytical nature, making personal development a journey steeped in self-discovery and spiritual exploration. This path emphasizes the importance of understanding one's inner self and the world around them. Life Path 7 encourages individuals to delve into their spiritual beliefs, fostering a connection with the universe that promotes growth and enlightenment. As they progress on this journey, it becomes crucial for these individuals to cultivate self-awareness, enabling them to navigate their unique challenges and harness their inherent gifts.

In the realm of spiritual growth, Life Path 7 individuals are naturally inclined to seek wisdom and knowledge. Their quest for understanding often leads them to explore various philosophical and spiritual teachings. Engaging with these concepts can serve as a catalyst for personal transformation, guiding them towards a deeper understanding of their purpose. This pursuit not only enhances their spiritual beliefs but also empowers them to align their actions with their values, ultimately leading to a more fulfilling life experience.

Finding a career that resonates with their inner calling is another vital aspect of personal development for Life Path 7 individuals. They thrive in environments that allow for independence and creativity, often gravitating towards roles that require analytical thinking and problem-solving skills. Whether it is in research, counseling, or the arts, Life Path 7 individuals are best suited for careers that challenge their intellect and provide opportunities for personal expression. By aligning their professional lives with their spiritual journey, they can unlock a sense of fulfillment that transcends traditional career satisfaction.

Relationships can pose unique challenges for Life Path 7 individuals, who often find themselves torn between their need for solitude and the desire for connection. Developing emotional intelligence is essential for navigating these dynamics, as it enables them to communicate effectively and understand the needs of others. By fostering strong relationships grounded in mutual respect and understanding, Life Path 7 individuals can create supportive networks that nurture both their spiritual and personal growth. This balance between introversion and social engagement is vital for their overall well-being.

Lastly, incorporating health and wellness practices into their daily routines can significantly enhance the personal development journey of Life Path 7 individuals. Mindfulness, meditation, and holistic health practices are particularly beneficial, as they help to ground their often introspective nature. These techniques not only promote emotional balance but also encourage creativity and self-expression, providing a holistic approach to their well-being. By integrating these practices into their lives, Life Path 7 individuals can overcome obstacles, fostering resilience and a deeper connection to their spiritual selves.

Chapter 12

Life Path 7: Balancing Introversion and Social Engagement

Understanding the Introverted Nature

Understanding the introverted nature of individuals on Life Path 7 is crucial for unlocking their potential and fostering spiritual growth. Introversion often manifests as a preference for solitude and reflection, providing Life Path 7 individuals with a rich inner world where they can explore their thoughts and feelings. This inward focus allows them to connect with their spiritual essence, enhancing their intuitive abilities and deepening their understanding of life's mysteries. Recognizing this trait helps individuals embrace their natural tendencies rather than forcing themselves into extroverted roles that may feel inauthentic or draining.

The introverted nature of Life Path 7 individuals can lead to unique challenges, particularly in social situations. While they may enjoy the company of others, prolonged social interactions can be overwhelming, which may result in feelings of anxiety or fatigue. Understanding this aspect of their personality is essential for navigating relationships and career paths. Life Path 7 individuals often excel in roles that allow for independent work, research, or creative expression, where they can utilize their analytical skills without the pressure of constant social engagement. By acknowledging their introversion, they can create environments that nurture their strengths.

Meditation and mindfulness practices are particularly beneficial for Life Path 7 individuals, as these techniques align with their introspective nature. Engaging in regular meditation allows them to cultivate a deeper sense of self-awareness and emotional intelligence. This practice can serve as a sanctuary, enabling them to recharge and reconnect with their spiritual journey. By incorporating meditation into their daily routine, they can enhance their ability to navigate the complexities of life while maintaining their inner peace.

Creativity and expression also flourish in the introverted space of Life Path 7 individuals. Their introspective tendencies often lead to profound insights, which can manifest in various forms of artistic expression. Whether through writing, painting, or music, these individuals can channel their thoughts and emotions into creative outlets that resonate deeply with their spiritual journey. Encouraging this creativity not only provides an avenue for self-expression but also contributes to their overall well-being, allowing them to process their experiences more effectively.

Balancing introversion with social engagement is a vital skill for Life Path 7 individuals to develop. While solitude is essential for their spiritual growth, finding opportunities to connect with like-minded individuals can enhance their personal development. Building meaningful relationships with others who understand their introverted nature can create a supportive network that fosters growth and collaboration. By learning to navigate social interactions in a way that honors their introverted tendencies, Life Path 7 individuals can thrive both personally and spiritually, unlocking the hidden gifts that their unique path offers.

Finding Balance in Social Interactions

Finding balance in social interactions is essential for individuals on Life Path 7, as they often navigate the delicate interplay between introspection and external engagement. Life Path 7 individuals are known for their analytical minds, deep spiritual inclinations, and a preference for solitude. While these traits can lead to profound insights and personal growth, they can also create challenges in social settings. Recognizing the importance of social interactions, Life Path 7 individuals must learn to balance their need for solitude with the need for connection, fostering relationships that support their spiritual journey.

Social interactions can serve as significant catalysts for personal development, particularly for those on Life Path 7. Engaging with others allows individuals to share their insights and learn from diverse perspectives. This exchange of ideas can be enriching, prompting self-reflection and growth. However, it is crucial for Life Path 7 individuals to identify their boundaries and understand when it is time to retreat into solitude. By establishing clear limits, they can protect their energy while still enjoying meaningful interactions that contribute to their overall well-being.

Emotional intelligence plays a vital role in finding balance in social interactions for Life Path 7 individuals. Developing this skill enables them to navigate complex social dynamics with grace and understanding. By honing their ability to empathize with others, Life Path 7 individuals can create deeper connections and foster a sense of belonging. At the same time, they must remain attuned to their own emotional needs, ensuring that their interactions do not drain their energy or compromise their spiritual focus. Striking this balance can lead to healthier, more fulfilling relationships.

Meditation and mindfulness practices can also support Life Path 7 individuals in achieving equilibrium in their social lives. These techniques provide a foundation for self-awareness, allowing individuals to recognize their emotional states and social preferences. Regular meditation can help Life Path 7 individuals cultivate a sense of inner peace, making it easier to engage with others when they choose to do so. By integrating these practices into their daily routines, they can manage stress and maintain a clear sense of purpose in their social interactions.

Ultimately, finding balance in social interactions is a continuous journey for those on Life Path 7. By embracing their unique gifts while remaining open to the insights gained from others, they can foster meaningful connections that enrich their lives. It is essential for Life Path 7 individuals to remember that social engagement does not have to compromise their spiritual path; rather, it can enhance their understanding of themselves and the world around them. By cultivating this balance, they can unlock the full potential of their life journey, leading to a more harmonious existence.

Building Meaningful Connections

Building meaningful connections is a critical aspect of the journey for individuals on Life Path 7, who often find themselves navigating the complexities of introspection and spirituality. Life Path 7 individuals are known for their analytical minds and deep quest for knowledge, which can sometimes lead to a sense of isolation. However, it is essential for them to recognize that building authentic relationships can significantly enhance their spiritual growth and emotional well-being. These connections not only provide support but also serve as mirrors, reflecting their inner journey and helping them understand themselves more profoundly.

To foster meaningful connections, Life Path 7 individuals must first embrace their unique qualities while being open to vulnerability. This can be a challenging task for those who are naturally private and introspective. Engaging in open conversations about their interests and passions can help bridge the gap between their inner world and the external environment. Sharing their experiences with like-minded individuals can lead to enriching exchanges that not only validate their perspectives but also encourage personal growth and exploration. Building trust and creating safe spaces for dialogue are essential steps in nurturing these relationships.

Additionally, Life Path 7 individuals should seek out communities that resonate with their spiritual pursuits. Joining groups focused on meditation, healing practices, or philosophical discussions can provide the necessary support and camaraderie. These environments often encourage individuals to express their thoughts and feelings freely, fostering a sense of belonging. Participation in workshops or retreats can also facilitate deeper connections, as such experiences often lead to shared insights and collective growth, reinforcing the idea that they are not alone on their spiritual journey.

Moreover, cultivating emotional intelligence is vital for Life Path 7 individuals as they navigate relationships. Understanding their own emotions and those of others can enhance their ability to connect on a deeper level. Practicing active listening, empathy, and non-judgmental communication can transform interactions into meaningful dialogues. By being present and genuinely interested in others' experiences, Life Path 7 individuals can forge bonds that are not only enriching but also grounded in mutual respect and understanding.

Lastly, balancing their inclination towards solitude with social engagement is crucial for Life Path 7 individuals. While introspection is a valuable aspect of their life path, it is essential to recognize the benefits of connecting with others. Setting aside time for social activities, whether attending events or simply reaching out to friends, can rejuvenate their spirits and provide fresh perspectives. By intentionally cultivating these connections, Life Path 7 individuals can unlock new dimensions of their spiritual journey, enriching their lives and the lives of those around them.